From the Mouth of Ma

A Search for Caroline Quiner Ingalls

Robynne Elizabeth Miller

DEDICATION

I dedicate this book to Lindsay, who first introduced me to the precious role of mother, to Hannah, who ignited in me a protectiveness and love I didn't know possible, to Nathan, who reminds me every day what fortitude is all about, to Seth, who changed my life in such a very short amount of time, and to Noah James, who still looks at me as if I am as awesome as Ma, even though I'm not.

I love you immeasurably, my babies. Sticky faces, and all.

Robynne Elizabeth Miller

CONTENTS

	Acknowledgments	vii
	A Note to Readers	ix
1	Who is Ma?	1
2	A Bit of Background	5
3	Wash on Monday. . .	9
4	Appearances are often Deceiving	13
5	Good Weather Never Lasts Forever	17
6	All's Well that Ends Well	21
7	Don't Cross a Bridge Until You Come to It	25
8	There's No Great Loss Without Some Gain	29
9	Better a Live Dog Than a Dead Lion Discretion is the Better Part of Valor	33
10	Don't Count Your Chickens Before They're Hatched	37
11	Pride Goes Before a Fall	41
12	We Must Cut Our Coat to fit Our Cloth	45
13	If wisdom's ways you wisely seek. . .	49
14	A Body Makes His Own Luck	55
15	Marry in Haste, Repent in Leisure Married in Black, You'll Wish Yourself Back	59
16	They That Dance Must Pay the Fiddler	65
	Conclusion	69

Robynne Elizabeth Miller

ACKNOWLEDGMENTS

Nothing worthwhile is ever accomplished without a community of support. I'm thankful I had such a community while working on this project.

My husband, Ian, gets the grandest thank-you! His willingness to give me the time and space to conduct hours of research and even more of writing was an unbelievable blessing. He has been an editor, researcher, encourager, critic, and cheerleader in the best of ways, and I am incredibly grateful for his unwavering support and belief in the writing passions that consume me.

My family, too, have been wonderful. Especially the three babies still at home who had to endure leftovers and some weekends without mom while all this was getting finished. Their belief in me, despite the fact that I am decidedly NOT like Ma, is one of my greatest blessings. Thank you Hannah, Nathan, and Noah James!

There are many more, too, who deserve thanks. . .my critique group ladies who endured a number of edits while steadfastly cheering me on, Janeane and Jason Wyatt who provided emergency research materials when I mistakenly left them at home, the Reno and Auburn librarians who helped me with random bits of research, and a countless number of friends who encouraged me through the process.

I am a lucky lady. Thank you all.

Robynne Elizabeth Miller

A NOTE TO READERS

Once upon a time, long, long ago, when I was a very little girl, I chose my first chapter book from the school library: *Little House in the Big Woods*, by Laura Ingalls Wilder. Before I had even opened to the first page, though, I was already hooked. The cover showed a darling brown haired girl, about my age, sweetly hugging a rag doll while, in the background, a loving family looked on. The snug log cabin scene seemed inviting, warm and, well, *idyllic*. A million miles away from my own troubled family's life in the modern suburbs.

A few years before I was old enough to start reading those chapter books, the Ingalls family made its way to Hollywood. I didn't meet them until years later (God bless reruns!!) but I quickly fell in love with them, too. Between Michael Landon's strong, devoted portrayal of Pa and Karen Grassle's gentle, warm depiction of Ma, I wished with all my might that I could pack up and move into the loft right next to Laura and Mary.

But even back then, young as I was, I knew that the *Little House* books and the *Little House* television series were not the same thing. Even I knew that Pa had a beard and rarely went about town shirtless, his rippling muscles glistening with sweat. And Ma wasn't prone to overt displays of affection or flirting with a passing handyman. Michael Landon and Karen Grassle could do these things in the make believe Walnut Grove. But Pa and Ma wouldn't in the real one.

Don't get me wrong. I loved them both. . .the books and the television show. But I knew, deeply, that they were only very tenuously connected. Kind of like the difference between Taco Bell and a really authentic Mexican restaurant. Or a vanilla scented air freshener and a fresh vanilla pod. I happen to love both, but I know they are not, really, the same thing.

And this distinction has been tricky for me over the years.

I'm a devoted fan of the *Little House* lineage. More toward the books and family history, but I do love both. I appreciate them in their uniqueness and for what each have brought to the world. But, in my mind, they don't cross. They shouldn't cross. They're separate. Completely and utterly separate.

So when someone finds out about my blogs or areas of study or books (mostly related to the real family and their prairie lifestyle), I always cringe a little. Stomach clenched, I wait to see if my new acquaintance is a kindred spirit, able to keep each *Little House* incarnation in its rightful place, or one of the many wonderful fans who, in my opinion, has things a little muddled up.

"Oh, I am a HUGE Little House buff," some have enthusiastically admitted. "I always wished Ma and Pa would adopt me like they did Albert and the others. Those books changed my life!"

Sigh. Ma and Pa never adopted anyone. Michael and Karen did on the TV show, but that never happened in real life.

So that's partially why I wanted to write this book. Karen Grassle was a talented actress who was brilliant as the TV Ma. But she wasn't the real Ma. And the real Ma is worth knowing, too.

There's not much written about her, though. And that's a pity. Maybe she wasn't as lively as Pa, with his bear hugs and fiddle playing, or as endearing as feisty tomboy, Laura, but she certainly is worth exploring in my opinion.

Teasing apart the real Ma from Karen Grassle's Ma can be difficult for those who've morphed them into one person over the years. But with utter respect for both Ma's, I hope this book will help to do just that.

CHAPTER 1

Who is Ma?

For those of us who've loved the Ingalls family from the first "Once Upon a Time" of *Little House in the Big Woods* right through to Laura's delightful discovery of her intricate new pantry in *These Happy Golden Years* (and beyond!), almost every "little house" resident seems like family. We bask in Pa's twinkling warmth and loving provision, Mary's patient and gentle goodness, despite tragically losing her sight, Carrie's sweet and worryingly delicate disposition, and even darling Grace's innocent blue eyes, framed beautifully by snowy swan's down. From Laura's detailed and tender description of her family's epic pioneer journey through the west, we've come to know them all well. . .or at least feel as though we deeply do.

But Ma has always felt like a bit of an enigma amongst all of those warm, familiar relations. On the one hand, Laura often described her as a gentle, loving woman who embodied the very essence of a perfect mother: quiet, patient, loving, capable and wise. That depiction appeared pleasant, reasonable and endearing enough. Though there were a few startling cracks in her seemingly flawless exterior, as well: her vehement hatred for all Indians[1], apparent disdain for "foreigners[2]," (despite the fact that her own grandparents arrived from Scotland as adults just two generations before), and uncharacteristic wish that Almanzo would break his own neck before he breaks Laura's while training wild horses[3]. Those rare blips aside, Ma's genteel character seemed largely

---

[1] Chapter 4, "Prairie Day," in *Little House on the Prairie*.
[2] Chapter 1, "Make Hay While the Sun Shines," in *The Long Winter*.
[3] Chapter 21, "Barnum and Skip," in *These Happy Golden Years*.

unblemished and certainly worth admiration.

Yet, I didn't feel like I *knew* her. At least not in the way I felt I should after more than a hundred delicious re-readings of the *Little House* series and devouring just about every other written thing pertaining to the Ingalls family.

That bothered me.

So, with great determination, I finally decided to ferret out the root of my odd sense of distance. Picking up my well-worn "reading" copies of the *Little House* series, I eagerly dove in. Paying careful attention to what Ma said and did, as well as to how she was characterized by Laura and others, I soon discovered something interesting: Ma is the only character in the series whose dialogue is rife with cliché's. *Absolutely rife.*

By the time I'd finished the eight *Little House* books that mention her (she's obviously not found in *Farmer Boy*!), I'd unearthed well more than twenty examples of Ma's "wisdom" being distilled in platitudes. Such sayings certainly have value and did fit the circumstance appropriately in every scene they appeared. But using such, well, almost *trite* nuggets really only serves to distance us from Ma. Instead of hearing Ma's insight flow from her own heart and in her own words, we are given commonplace phrases and proverbs! How can we learn who Ma really was from that? Without Ma's own fears, beliefs, hopes, thoughts and words saturating each interaction Laura wrote about, Ma remains slightly veiled and somewhat out of focus.

As a result, we don't feel quite the same intimacy we do with Laura herself, nor with Pa, who might wrap us up in a big bear hug at any moment or lift us tenderly into a wagon. No, we feel a slight formal distance between us and this stoic pioneer woman, as if we must make sure to cross our legs at the ankles and be extra careful not to spill our tea when we meet her.

Perhaps this written emotional distance was merely a

reflection of Laura's own relationship with her mother. Her writings clearly demonstrate that she idolized her father and was careful to keep his many missteps and penchant for dragging the family to and fro on a moment's notice out of her loving narrative of their family adventures. Don't get me wrong, though. . .I think it's clear that she both loved and respected her mother a great deal, as well. But Laura definitely leaned toward her Pa, clearly preferring to help with mixing mud plaster for the chimney or making stout oak doors with no nails to quietly sewing quilt patches inside the stuffy cabin with her Ma.

So that may be the innocent answer to it all: Laura spent a lot more quality time with her father, and certainly admitted to having a decidedly tomboyish bent, so it stands to reason that she knew and related to him far better and, therefore, could represent him with more endearing accuracy.

Or perhaps it has nothing to do with Laura's personality and obvious affection for her father at all. Perhaps Caroline was merely one of those kind, yet formal and distant, people whose façade even close family members could not fully penetrate.

Either way, Laura's decision to write less about her mother than her father in general and then, when she did, to revert to clichés, speaks loudly to me. Instead of leaving me happy to keep Caroline at a respectful arm's length, however, it leaves me hungry to know more of her than Laura was able (or willing!) to convey.

I'd love to sit down with Caroline, perhaps over some rich vanity cakes and sweet ginger tea, to get to know her better. But, obviously, that's not an option. Except for a few historical mentions here and there, as well as the broadly fictionalized portrayal of her young life in *The Caroline Years*, clichés are what we got, so clichés are what we'll work with.

But what on earth can we glean about Ma from a couple dozen time-worn platitudes? A lot, if we care to look. Which I do.

If you do, too, read on. Perhaps we'll both get to know Ma a little better along the way!

CHAPTER 2

A Bit of Background

Before we delve straight into deconstructing Ma's litany of clichés, and seeing if we can gain a little insight into this fascinating woman, it's probably a good idea to briefly run through her background. After all, she didn't just materialize out of thin air at the beginning of *Little House in the Big Woods*, now, did she?

Caroline Lake Quiner was born in the little town of Brookfield, Wisconsin, on December 12, 1839 to Henry and Charlotte Quiner. She was their fifth child, though only her two older brothers, Joseph and Henry, and older sister, Martha, were alive at that time. After Caroline, Henry and Charlotte had two more children: Eliza and Thomas.

Sadly, Caroline's beloved father was lost in a boating accident on Lake Michigan just a month before her sixth birthday. I can't imagine the grief such a very little girl would have experienced during this kind of tragedy. Though young, Caroline was old enough to understand the implications of his death, both financial and emotional, and to mourn deeply. I believe this event had a profound and lasting effect on her, as it would anybody.

But I believe that the next several years were even more important in the formation of Caroline's lasting core values. As her newly widowed mother struggled to support and care for her large family, every child, even young Caroline, needed to grow up quickly, function as a cooperative unit and do their best to contribute to the family's success. That's a heavy burden for any child to carry. But, by all accounts, she did her part, and did so willingly.

After Henry's death, the family remained in Brookfield for a short time until Caroline's mother, Charlotte, decided to move them all to a rugged piece of land in the more remote (and less expensive) burgh of Concord (Jefferson County, Wisconsin). She was simply in search of a better, and more sustainable, life for her brood. They could start this life on land they owned, rather than the Brookfield piece they did not. But the family continued to struggle as they contrived to keep everyone fed, clothed and well while they carved out their new home in an undeveloped patch of rough woods.

A few years later, Caroline's mother married Frederick Holbrook, with whom she had one more daughter, also named Charlotte. This union eased their tenuous financial situation greatly, but the years between Henry's death and Charlotte's re-marriage were difficult for the heartbroken family and undeniably impacted them all.

Yet, I believe something powerful was birthed there during that lean, frightening period: a deep sense of realistic practicality, a profound understanding of the difference between "wants" and "needs," and a beautifully stoic resilience in the face of loss and difficulties.

These themes followed Caroline as she left home for the first time to finish her education, returned to her family to start teaching in Concord at age sixteen, and then began her life with family friend and neighbor, Charles Ingalls, marrying him on February 1, 1860. At each step, Caroline demonstrated her bent toward living sensibly and efficiently in the present, her understanding of the value of money and what it could and could not buy, and an innate ability to flourish under even incredibly stressful circumstances.

Right through Laura's *Little House* books, these themes further deepened. After the death of Caroline's father, the family learned to live in the moment. . .not worrying about what was ahead, but choosing to meet the day's trouble without complaint or self-pity. As Caroline moved into adult married life with Charles and experienced enormous financial, health, and emotional difficulties, this enduring woman pushed forward with calm resolve and pragmatism. Her early years had forged in her a sort of gentle strength and almost fatalistic perspective.

> "This earthly life is a battle," said Ma. "If it isn't one thing to contend with, it's another. It always has been so, and it always will be. The sooner you make up your mind to that, the better off you are, and the more thankful for your pleasures."[4]

Throughout the *Little House* books, and, by all accounts, throughout her life, Caroline remained practical, pragmatic, and without a hint of self-pity.

But Caroline did more than merely stoically endure her life. She chose to be *grateful* for whatever she had and in whatever circumstance befell the family. I find this her most endearing quality. Though there were several significant opportunities for bitterness or grumbling throughout the *Little House* narratives, Caroline was never portrayed as complaining about lack of luxuries, or even necessities. I'm not sure I could have been so consistently thankful!

> "Don't complain, Laura!" Ma told her quickly. "Never complain of what you have. Always remember you are fortunate to have it."[5]

Nor was she ever depicted as emotionally collapsing when deep losses or tragedies occurred: grasshopper plagues, the "Hard Winter," loss of homes, drought, illness, etc. No, Caroline had a

---

[4] Chapter 9, "Blackbirds," in *Little Town on the Prairie*.
[5] Chapter 23, "The Wheat in the Wall," in *The Long Winter*.

quiet strength, most likely modeled by her own strong and resilient mother and, again, honed in the sad, lean years of struggle after her father's death.

Caroline remained calm, practical, and matter of fact about whatever circumstance her family found themselves in. . .always ready to do her part to insure the family's success without drama or tantrums.

In my opinion, these core qualities made her particularly suitable to marry a man like Pa. Not many other women would have had the fortitude to endure both his endless wanderings as well as nature's destructive curve balls! Especially without complaining!

So this is the Caroline we're going to look for amongst a selection of clichés and platitudes. This is the *Ma* we're going to seek. There, amidst well-worn adages, we'll hunt for her humanity. We'll hunt for her motivations. And we'll hunt for her heart.

Ready? Let's go!

CHAPTER 3

Wash on Monday,
Iron on Tuesday,
Mend on Wednesday,
Churn on Thursday,
Clean on Friday,
Bake on Saturday,
Rest on Sunday

In the first chapter of Laura's book, *Little House in the Big Woods*, we get a glimpse of the family's home, land, fall chores and Pa's personality. Pa engages in lively dialogue, is lovingly described, and has multiple interactions with Laura and Mary. Ma, on the other hand, does not. Ma doesn't really get a mention, nor even a real appearance, except to be named as a resident of the little house and as the recipient of some good fresh venison that Pa provides, until she's tasked with putting some green hickory chips on the small fire while smoking the remaining venison for winter.

She's there, though, in that first chapter. . .quietly milling about in the background, doing daily chores and keeping her family fed. None of it is "front row" stuff, though, and mostly reminds us that Ma is the heart of the home. After her mention with the smoker, for example, we get to "see" her trying out lard in a big iron pot, making headcheese and sausage, and then unobtrusively receding into the shadows again while jovial Pa greases traps and entertains Laura and Mary with exciting, lively stories.

Even into the second chapter, we don't get any direct glimpse of Ma's personality until she's reported to have said that "Jack Frost came in the night and made the pictures, while everyone was asleep."[6]

Whimsical? Yes! Despite the rather removed way of attributing this thought to her (via third person, rather than direct dialogue, like Laura had been doing with Pa), we learn that Ma does have a slightly fanciful side. That charming winter image, faint though it is, does not last long, however. . .we turn the page and, already, it's chore time again!

That Ma adhered to the structure of "Wash on Monday," is not particularly remarkable. It was a fairly commonplace practice at that time. There are two thoughts on the rhyme's origin, though both are closely related. The first is that the concept came from England, where the order of the chores simply made practical sense (washing the clothes first, then ironing the resulting clean clothes, then mending what you discovered needed fixing during the washing/ironing phase, etc.).

The second possible origin is based on a combination of this sensible English practice of logically setting out each weekday's task and the fact that the very first thing the Pilgrim women did after coming ashore on Monday, November 13, 1620, was to wash their months-old filthy clothes. (Can you imagine 68 days at sea worth of dirt?! Yuck!!) This took the English tradition and set it on a new timescale, firmly tying the pattern of tasks to specific days of the week rather than just a rhythmic cycle you could start almost any day.

Not everyone followed the rhyme's structure, however. Later in *Little House in the Big Woods*, when Pa takes the family to the town of Pepin, Laura sees that "Though it was not Monday, some woman had spread out a washing on the bushes and stumps by her house."[7]

---

[6] Chapter 2, "Winter Days and Winter Nights," in *Little House in the Big Woods*.
[7] Chapter 9, "Going to Town," in *Little House in the Big Woods*.

Still, it wasn't unusual for Ma to follow the tradition or the rhyme. It made good sense and it provided a practical, logical, and ordered structure on which she could hang her week.

So what do the first couple of chapters of *Little House in the Big Woods*, culminating with our first lengthy scenes of the family doing the ordered chores of the week, reveal about Ma? I'd like to think that is shows her leanings toward sensible household structure, practicality, and that she seemed to take her duties as a housewife and mother pretty seriously.

It's a little too early in the series to read too much into the fact that Ma is mostly relegated to the background of these first chapters of the book and series, with no significant personal interaction or dialogue, but let's file that bit away and see if it pops up anywhere else.

For now, it's enough to know that Ma was a hard worker, liked order, and carried out her many homemaking responsibilities efficiently and without complaint. I don't think my own children could honestly write the same about me!

Robynne Elizabeth Miller

CHAPTER 4

Appearances are often Deceiving

I've often wondered where the phrase "Appearances are Deceiving" comes from, but never really bothered to take the time to look it up. After all, the meaning of it is pretty straightforward, even if you don't know its origin: things aren't always as they seem to be.

The phrase, and variations thereof, comes from one of Aesop's fables, "The Wolf in Sheep's Clothing," in which a wolf, having trouble getting at a flock of sheep, finds a sheepskin and puts it on. Now *looking* like a sheep, he easily infiltrates the unsuspecting flock, devouring them at will. Moral? Appearances can, indeed, be deceiving. (And dangerous, too!)

When Ma utters these words, there appears to be no particular motivation for this kind of lesson. Laura and Mary are simply helping her with the summer chore of making cheese when Ma slips this little nugget into the conversation. She's not using it to moralize about any current situation. She's not correcting the girls or passing judgment on a person or situation that embodies this concept. She just tosses it in while she wipes the green cheeses and rubs them with fresh butter to create a hard rind.

So why did Laura attribute this random phrase to her mother, and, more importantly, what does this reveal about Ma?

Despite Ma's earlier nod to the Jack Frost tale, and even her mention here that "the moon is made of green cheese, some people say,"[8] I don't think Ma was being particularly imaginative or even attempting to be entertaining or engaging with her girls. I think Laura was giving an example of Ma's bent toward teaching her children practical and social lessons during every day chores

---

[8] Chapter 10, "Summertime," in *Little House in the Big Woods*.

and projects.

Ma appears more to be creating an opportunity to make a distinction between the fanciful notions of some people and the value of plain facts. When Laura wonders if "the moon is really made of green cheese," Ma sensibly replies that she thinks "people say that, because it looks like a green cheese." She then quickly takes the opportunity to slip in a significant life lesson, which I believe was her real intention: "But appearances are deceiving."[9]

This last short and concise conclusion is important. Ma was using a wide-spread whimsical notion to drive home a simple idea: Don't get caught up in a romantic, emotional response to a person or thing or situation. Look practically behind the façade and see what truth lies there. To put it even more bluntly: Think with your head, not your heart!

Ma didn't appear to have a lot of time for folly or imaginations. She was a hard-working wife and mother, and she wanted to make sure her children guarded themselves against flights of fancy and kept their feet squarely on the ground. So it makes sense that, instead of stories or jokes or other seemingly unnecessary entertainments during work time, Ma chose to couple practical chores with important life lessons.

But is that all Ma might have meant through her quick, short lesson on appearances? Maybe. Or there may be a little more.

In a letter dated October 6, 1861, Ma (before she was a mother!) strangely encourages her older sister, Martha, who has just had a baby, to "strive to bring him up to be an honor to his parents and his country."[10] I say "strangely" because Ma is

---

[9] Chapter 10, "Summertime," in *Little House in the Big Woods*.

[10] Quiner Ingalls, Caroline. "Letter to Martha Quiner Carpenter, Oct. 6, 1861." Wisconsin Historical Society. http://content.wisconsinhistory.org/cdm/ref /collection/tp/id/44380.

younger than Martha by a couple of years, has no children of her own yet, and is only newly married herself. Not exactly the wizened platform from which you'd expect such formal advice to flow.

Yet Ma's childhood troubles show through here: She's mature beyond her years and is confident in her matter-of-fact opinions. To bring honor to your parents and country could mean a million things, of course. But Ma valued honesty and forthrightness deeply. So I think that, at least in part, she was encouraging her older sister to bring up her son to be a what-you-see-is-what-you-get kind of fellow. . .one who is honest, practical, dependable, and a credit to those around him.

I don't know how you'd feel if someone gave you advice on a subject they had no firsthand experience of, especially if that someone was your younger, less experienced, sibling, but I'm always a little leery of advice from such folks. I prefer hearing time-tested wisdom distilled from the been-there-done-that crowd, for the most part. Yet, I think that Ma's values were so clear to her, and so simple and non-negotiable, that it isn't unreasonable to reconcile the before-children-came Ma with the mother of three's unwavering assertion that we should make sure to portray ourselves honestly and with honor as well as to take great care not to get emotionally caught up in the fanciful deceptions of another.

Isn't that refreshing? Our modern world seems populated with people trying to impress and outdo each other, sometimes untruthfully. So the thought of living in a community of simple, honest, above board kind of folks like Ma is particularly attractive. At least to me!

Robynne Elizabeth Miller

CHAPTER 5

Good Weather Never Lasts Forever

It's funny that I can't find any direct historical reference to this particular quote of Ma's. Funny because my own grandmother used to say it often, as did a childhood teacher of mine. I guess I've just always assumed that it was another standard cliché "old folks" would pull out to rain on whatever current parade us kids happened to be enjoying.

Despite no (as yet unearthed) direct reference, however, there's plenty of internet speculation that it's just an informal interpretation of one of two Biblical passages: either Matthew 24 or Ecclesiastes 3. The passage in Matthew seems more often linked to similar phrases, but I'm not at all convinced. It says, in part, "You will hear of wars and rumors of wars, but see to it that you are not alarmed. Such things must happen, but the end is still to come."[11]

If I squint and look sideways, I can see a tentative link between Ma's statement that "good weather never lasts forever on this earth"[12] and the idea that all things will eventually pass away. But I think that the far likelier connection is with the passage from Ecclesiastes, which begins, "There is a time for everything, and a season for every activity under the heavens."[13]

Doesn't that seem to fit a little better?

It's no stretch at all to imagine Ma paraphrasing a concept from the Bible. She was a devout Christian who studied and memorized Scripture throughout her long lifetime. As the passage in Ecclesiastes directly speaks about the cycles and cadence of life,

---

[11] Matt. 24:6.

[12] Chapter 8, "Two Stout Doors," in *Little House on the Prairie*.

[13] Eccl. 3:1.

I'd bet the farm it's what she had in mind whenever she used this phrase.

The second verse of that chapter goes on to note that there's "a time to be born and a time to die, a time to plant and a time to uproot," which are, of course, direct references to the phases of life and of seasons. I can't imagine a more perfect source for Ma's statement.

Ma was a pragmatist. She knew that seasons came and went whether she wanted them to or not. So whether she actually uttered these words, or merely lived the concept out, Laura was clearly reminding us of Ma's general disposition when she placed this adage into her mouth. Ma wasn't a rest-on-your-laurels kind of gal. She took life as it came, good or bad, knowing that good times usually came to an end, just as bad ones did, if you were patient long enough. There was no use in trying to fight either. And it was best to be prepared for both!

By not corrupting Ma's practical view of things with even a hint of regret or self-pity, however, Laura told us something more: Ma's character was pretty darn tough. Did that mean she had an icy personality, keeping her true feelings bottled up inside? Perhaps. She sure didn't seem to believe in overt displays of emotion, either in word or deed.

Or, as I prefer to think, did Ma merely learn, at a very tender age, to gracefully accept every twist and turn life could throw at a person, without fuss or self-pity? This was a far more dignified prospect than trying to fight fate tooth and nail and not changing a blessed little thing in the end, anyway. And I think it sums Ma up pretty darn well.

In an undated letter, probably from around 1938, from Laura to her daughter, Rose Wilder Lane, Laura explains more about the family dynamic:

> We were not excitable, usually Pa sometimes and Laura now and then. I don't think Ma ever was. She would not be. . .It seems to me we were rather inclined to be … to just take things as they came. I know we all hated a fuss, as I still do.[14]

That seems to fit well with what we're learning, doesn't it? Not only are we getting confirmation about Ma's stoic personality, but we're also getting a hint again about Laura and Ma's relationship. If Laura didn't "think Ma ever was" excited, she didn't really know for sure, did she? This seems to show a slight lack of intimacy.

We also see from Laura's description that Ma "would not be" excited. As a redheaded Northern California mountain girl, I can attest to the fact that I don't always have such tight control over my emotions. Especially excitement! That Ma clearly had is almost mind-boggling to me.

As I mentioned in an earlier chapter, Ma reminds Laura in *Little Town on the Prairie* that

> this earthly life is a battle. . .If it isn't one thing to contend with, it's another. It always has been so, and it always will be. The sooner you make up your mind to that, the better off you are, and the more thankful for your pleasures."[15]

Though some might disagree, that doesn't sound like a pessimist or defeatist to me. That sounds like someone who

---

[14] Whitlock, Cheryl. "Letters from Laura." Beyond Little House. April 15, 2009. http://beyondlittlehouse.com/2009/04/15/letters-from-laura/.
[15] Chapter 9, "Blackbirds," in *Little Town on the Prairie*.

learned young to take life as it came, the good and the bad together—knowing they both are transient—and to be intentionally grateful for each and every blessing along the way.

Personally, I think that's a powerful lesson for us all!

CHAPTER 6

All's Well that Ends Well

Given the fact that the *Little House* books were written by a schoolteacher AND Ma, herself, was a schoolteacher at one point, we knew Shakespeare would probably get a nod at some point, now didn't we? Old Will is certainly credited with the saying "All's well that ends well!" often enough, having used it as the title of a play he wrote in 1601. But, actually, the saying significantly pre-dated him!

John Heywood (another literary fellow Shakespeare would have been aware of) gets the earliest written credit, when he included it in *"A dialogue conteinyng the nomber in effect of all the prouerbes in the Englishe tongue,"* in 1546. The mention comes here:

> Lovers live by love, ye as larkes live by leekes
> Saied this Ales, muche more then halfe in mockage.
> Tushe (quoth mine aunte) these lovers in dotage
> Thinke the ground beare them not, but wed of corage
> They must in all haste, though a leafe of borage
> Might by all the substance that they can fell.
> Well aunt (quoth Ales) all is well that ends well.[16]

Since Mr. Heywood was only writing down the English proverbs already popularly circulating in the 1500's, it's no surprise that the maxim was ingrained into the public vernacular enough to have jumped the pond with the pilgrims and make its way into everyday conversation way out there on the prairie. I'd

---

[16] Martin, Gary. "All's Well That Ends Well - Meaning and Origin." The Phrase Finder. http://www.phrases.org.uk/meanings/29800.html.

like to believe that Ma was well read enough to have gleaned it from Shakespeare directly but, more probably, it was just a commonly used phrase. What feels uncommon to me, however, is the almost cavalier way Ma is portrayed to have used it.

In *Little House on the Prairie*, a roaring grass fire comes whooshing across the countryside toward the Ingalls' homestead. Ma and Pa race to plow a thin fire break around the house and barn, quickly light a backfire on the other side of the furrow as even more of a barrier, and attempt to put out all of the flames that jump across the break and head toward the house. After a tremendous and frantic amount of work, fear, and luck, the fire passes them by without any real harm done. Ma then comes back to the "house to wash her hands and face. She was all streaked with smoked and sweat, and she was trembling."[17]

Instead of being shown to comfort her terrified young daughters, or even take a moment to rest and gather herself after the emotional and frightening ordeal, Ma simply cleans up and moves on. She remarks, calmly, that "there was nothing to worry about. 'The backfire saved us.'" She follows that up with a matter-of-fact "and all's well that ends well."

What?!?!

I like to think of myself as a reasonably positive person, and I get that Ma had already survived (and been toughened by) many tragedies and challenges throughout her life. But her response to this event was puzzling. It could have killed her whole family, burned their home to ashes, obliterated wild food sources and destroyed all of their provisions, livestock, transportation, and various other earthly possessions. This would have left them stranded there on the prairie in the middle of nowhere. . .so Ma's response just doesn't compute.

---

[17] Chapter 22, "Prairie Fire," in *Little House on the Prairie*.

Where's the appropriate fear response? Where's the comforting of very young children who've just been legitimately scared out of their wits? Where's the humble gratefulness for being spared any real damage? Why does Ma suddenly seem, well, almost plastic, icy, and more distant than ever?

There's a combination of things at play here. One is that Laura is probably attempting to keep the literary character of Ma consistent. . .she's practical, not prone to getting excited about much (see quote in Chapter 5 to confirm!), and just tends to roll with life's punches. Yes, this is a particularly dramatic event, which could have had catastrophic results, but Ma's response, filtered through Laura's perception, is consistent with the Ma we've come to know and that Laura was developing in her novels.

But there's something else, there, too. Laura was deliberate about describing the emotion and import of the fire. She used words like "running, galloping, shouted, bounding, hurry!, leaping, wildly, screaming, thrashed, roaring, flaring, twisting, blazed, squealing, whirling, crackling, rushing, and shriek" to describe the movement and terror and ferocity and utter drama of the scene. We were left in no doubt that this was a terrifying event to a child. As it would, of course, have been to anyone.

Of her own response to the scene's chaos, Laura writes that "she wanted to do something, but inside her head was a roaring and whirling like the fire. Her middle shook, and tears poured out of her stinging eyes. Her eyes and her nose and her throat stung with smoke."[18]

Does that sound like someone you'd pass up on the way to the washstand? My Mama's heart breaks for little Laura here. No mention of any maternal affection, compassion, or comfort at all. None of Pa's great big bear hugs or encouraging words (he's likely

---

[18] Chapter 22, "Prairie Fire," in *Little House on the Prairie*.

at the barn, putting up and caring for the horses after his emergency plowing effort). In fact, there is no direct communication at all. Just a frightened little girl left to cope on her own. But even all those years later, when she came to write of this event as an older woman, Laura didn't express pain or anger toward Ma in what she wrote. Though, I wonder if it was there in what she didn't.

I struggle with this scene. I have four children, the youngest of whom is right in the age range that Laura and Mary were during the fire. I've seen my children scared and my maternal instinct is ALWAYS to comfort and calm them, even in the midst of handling the crisis. So it's hard to think of Laura's mother choosing to just walk past her young daughters and go get cleaned up instead. If there is any truth to Laura's perception of this event, what an impact that must have made on her tender young heart.

The fire, thankfully, didn't ravage their lives or possessions, nor did anyone get physically injured. But I have to wonder whether Ma's strange response, or lack thereof, did damage far beyond the reaches of the flames.

And whether all was really well after all.

CHAPTER 7

Don't Cross a Bridge Until You Come to It

Also probably English in origin (do we see a theme there, as well?), this proverb didn't get a written mention until Ma was about ten or eleven years old. Henry Wadsworth Longfellow's "The Golden Legend" (published in 1851) states: "Don't cross the bridge till you come to it, is a proverb old and of excellent wit." So it was clearly in general circulation for quite a while by the time Ma was said to have uttered it at approximately thirty-five years old. And of all the platitudes that Laura attributed to her throughout the *Little House* books, this phrase seems to sum Ma up most succinctly.

Why? Because it seemed to be the mantra that permeated her life and countenance!

The proverb doesn't make sense if you read it literally. I mean, who can cross a bridge they haven't even come to yet? Impossible! But, like many proverbs and old sayings, its underlying meaning is simple and straightforward: Don't worry about something until it actually happens.

Ma's strong Christian faith was probably behind this belief as well. A popular Biblical passage in Matthew she would have been well familiar with says: "Therefore do not worry about tomorrow, for tomorrow will worry about itself. Each day has enough trouble of its own."[19] And, boy, wasn't that the darn truth for the Ingalls?

By the time this quote is attributed to Ma, the family had left the Big Woods, wandered for weeks into Kansas, endured injury, fire, threat of massacre, thieving of their food and other possessions, been evicted from their homestead, and nearly had an

---

[19] Matt. 6:34 NIV.

ox come through their thatched dugout roof! And that's just some of the milder stuff Laura deemed tame enough to make it into her *Little House* narrative! So it's quite apparent that there was enough rubbish to deal with on Ma's daily plate, without worrying about something that may or may not eventually come to pass!

In those lean, difficult years after her father's death, Ma and her family knew hunger and want. Intimately. By necessity, each day required complete focus and attention and effort just to survive. Worrying about next year, next month, or even next week just wasn't their priority, particularly when pressing chores needed to be done and their tummies were grumbling from hunger right that very minute!

Once you get into a particular mindset, it typically stays put unless something significant wrenches it out. I don't think Ma's early stance on this concept ever did leave her. She confronted each of life's challenges with grace, dignity and a fatalistic calm. No use in struggling against the inevitable, after all!

And I have to agree, there is wisdom there. . .significant wisdom. . .in not getting too ahead of yourself and worrying about something that may not even come to pass. Or be a problem if it does. My trouble is with the timing of Ma's quote here to her young daughter, Laura. If we look closely enough, we can see faint echoes of the concerns we had over the lack of Ma's maternal warmth after the prairie fire.

In this scene, Laura is supposed to be six. Later in *On the Banks of Plum Creek*, in Chapter 19: The Fish Trap, Ma chides Laura because "a great girl almost eight years old should be learning to read instead of running wild." But Laura wouldn't have been "almost eight years old" at this point. Laura turned seven in February and they went to school in late spring, when the wheat field was only pale green and silky. So she wasn't even seven and a half. (I get the feeling that the day after your birthday, you were "going on" whatever year was next!!) The Christmas before, then, she would have still been only six. And six is pretty little.

My youngest child is currently eight. I'm pretty sure this is the last year he'll sort of believe in Santa Claus. He might pretend to next year, just to appease me, but this year, he's a bit on the fence about whether Father Christmas is real. But, two years ago? Absolutely certain! No question about it! The cloudy facts surrounding St. Nick's ability to fit inside all sizes of chimneys (especially without becoming covered in soot) or to travel to every house on earth in just one night (when it takes us a whole day just to fly back to England for a paternal family visit!) notwithstanding, he was without reservation about the existence of Father Christmas at six!

So it stands to reason that Laura would have been fairly certain of Santa Claus, too. And, if she was, her angst over their current living situation would have been, to such a young child, both real and worrisome.

> Then Laura had a chance to speak without interrupting. She said, 'There isn't any fireplace.'
> 'Whatever are you talking about?' Ma asked her.
> 'Santa Claus,' Laura answered.[20]

Without any apparent understanding of (or concern for??) her young daughter's real-to-her worries about this, Ma simply replies:

> Eat your supper, Laura, and let's not cross

---

[20] Chapter 12, "The Christmas Horses," in *On the Banks of Plum Creek*.

bridges till we come to them.

That doesn't seem particularly warm or compassionate, now does it? Just a short while later, Ma debunks the whole Santa myth altogether in an attempt to encourage the girls to wish only for family work horses for Christmas instead of anything for themselves.

I don't think that Ma was intending to be harsh or unkind to her daughters. After all, Ma's eyes were tragically and abruptly opened to the stark realities of life when she was only five herself. Laura has made it to nearly seven years old without too much personal tragedy, but I believe this scene and quote succinctly depicts Ma's overall personality and core beliefs: Needs over wants. Reality over fancies. Practicality over luxuries.

I wish Ma had done it more gently. It's hard enough to think of that moment a child's belief system in things like Santa and the tooth fairy are shattered. Especially little Laura, whom we've all come to love. If it had to happen, I wish that Ma had wrapped her up in a big hug like Pa might have as she broke the news. But even if I don't really like the delivery much, I can, at least, agree with Ma's wisdom.

Most of us have quite enough to deal with on a daily basis without looking for more in tomorrow. With the twists and turns of life so frequent and surprising, it's really wasted energy we spend when planning for, or responding to, something that hasn't happened yet. Ma didn't waste anything, including effort and emotion. She pressed on with what was right in front of her.

I can almost hear her admonishing us from out there on the prairie. . . "If we get to that bridge," she might say, "we'll cross it then. But for today, well, it has quite enough trouble of its own!"

CHAPTER 8

There's No Great Loss Without Some Gain

Lest we get too down on Ma for possible maternal failings, I'm glad we get to head quickly down another trail. This particular saying is one of my personal favorites out of the whole *Little House* series. Not only is it something I heard frequently from various relatives in my childhood, but it's also been a principle I've tried to incorporate into my own life through the years. Although I can't be certain just when and where this nugget took hold of me, I'd like to think that Ma gets the full credit for planting this little gem.

Life is hard and full of bumps and bruises and unexpected losses. Being able to find something positive to hold onto during dark, difficult moments has often helped pull me out of life's mire and restore a bit of hope even when all hope seemed lost.

But, then again, I'm an emotional, romantic redhead slightly bent toward the dramatic.

I'm not sure that Ma was drawn to the emotional, idealistic side of the phrase like I am. Likely she was more attracted to its plain, matter of fact, sensible nature. After all, torrential rain means you don't need to water your lawn! A broken leg means you have time to read and won't wear out your shoes so fast! And a raging prairie fire makes it much easier to plow the thick grasslands! Right?

Nearest I can figure out, this old proverb is Italian in origin (for a change!).[21],[22] Unsurprisingly, it means exactly what it seems to: no matter what calamity befalls you, there's some tiny bit of good that usually accompanies the bad. Looking for that good in

---

[21] "Italian Proverbs." http://funsms.org/proverbs_italian.php.

[22] Stone, Jon R. *The Routledge Book of World Proverbs*. Routledge, 2006. 267.

the modern day is often an overlooked art. We want our apples to be flawless, our homes to look like magazines, and our relationships to be easy and always enjoyable. We don't tend to "do" difficulty or imperfections very well as a society. Nor do we seem to tolerate them well in our own lives.

But Ma did. And that is squarely to her credit.

I don't know that anyone would blame Ma if an early seed of bitterness had taken root. A series of difficulties and tragedies begun in childhood (and continuing well into adulthood!) would probably crush us rather self-indulged pantywaists today. We've certainly lost a lot of the fortitude and pluck and practicality our forefathers seemed to have by the bucketsful. Yet Ma did not become bitter after each unpleasant twist of fate or happenstance. Instead, she simply became more and more pragmatic as the years marched on.

But the best kind of pragmatism comes with at least a small touch of optimism. And I'd like to think Ma had that, too.

When the catastrophic grasshopper plague of the mid 1870's descended, the Ingalls' fortunes took a swift and ugly nose-dive. Rocky Mountain Locusts came in thick, shimmering clouds by the billions upon billions (and yes, I said BILLIONS) to consume every edible thing in their path.

In an article called *When The Skies Turned To Black, The Locust Plague of 1875,* Hearthstone Legacy Publications notes that:

> Lush gardens and fields of a wide range of crops were reduced to a barren, desert like appearance within a matter of hours. Crops that were needed to sustain a family and their farm animals were destroyed leaving no means of support during

the coming winter.[23]

The article notes that the swarm was estimated to have been approximately 1,800 miles long and 110 miles wide. That's 198,000 square miles (bigger than the states of California and South Carolina combined!) of chomping, insatiable bugs eating every green thing they could find.

The Ingalls' yields were not spared. A year's worth of food for the family, winter fodder for the stock, and sellable crops meant to meet the never-ending obligations of taxes and shoes and store bought necessities and even seeds for next year were gone in a matter of hours. All the money needed to plant the crops, and the hundreds of hours of time and effort to till, sow, and tend the harvest, were obliterated in a matter of moments.

With that kind of overwhelming devastation, there are not many people who would begrudge the Ingalls family a moment to indulge in a bit of self-pity. I'd hazard a guess that many modern folks might pitch a tent right there in the midst of defeatism and depression and stay put. But the Ingalls didn't. *Ma didn't.*

Pa headed east to look for work and Ma soldiered on at the farm while he did. Pa might be away, the year's crops devastated, and the scenery annihilated, but, you know what? The abundance of grasshoppers meant some bit of good:

> "Well, we won't need to buy feed for the hens," said Ma. "There's no great loss without some gain."[24]

---

[23] "When The Skies Turned To Black: The Locust Plaque of 1875." Hearthstone Legacy Publications. http://www.hearthstonelegacy.com/when-the-skies-turned-to-black-the_locust-plague-of-1875.htm.

[24] Chapter 25, "The Glittering Cloud," in *On the Banks of Plum Creek.*

Tiny gain? Perhaps.

But Ma saw it.

And, bless her, it gave her enough courage to go on.

CHAPTER 9

Better a Live Dog Than a Dead Lion
Discretion is the Better Part of Valor

I was a little shocked to find that the first of these two proverbs is actually another Scripture reference! (don't tell my college Old Testament professor!!) It certainly goes with Ma's penchant for Bible-based wisdom, though! It's from Ecclesiastes again:

> Anyone who is among the living has hope --even a live dog is better off than a dead lion![25]

The verse is pretty self-explanatory: Death is a pretty final situation. It's better to use your wisdom to stay alive than to rashly die in the arbitrary name of honor.

The second is another nod to Shakespeare who, in *Henry IV, Part One*, 1596, has his character, Falstaff, distill the following wisdom:

> The better part of valour is discretion; in the which better part I have saved my life.[26]

To understand this quote better, it may help to replace a couple of the words. Valor could be defined as bravery. Discretion is a concise word for a wise decision. So the gist of the idea is that making a wise, thoughtful decision in any circumstance is better than simply behaving rashly, albeit bravely.

When Ma uttered these two phrases in close proximity in *By the Shores of Silver Lake*, it clearly shocked young Laura. Pa was calmly relaying the story of a nearby railroad paymaster who chose to give an angry, irrational, murderous mob the up-to-the-minute pay they were demanding (but had not yet received funds

---

[25] Eccl. 9:4 NIV.
[26] *Henry IV, Part 1*, V, iv.

for) rather than risk his own life in denying their raucous and unreasonable request.

Laura declared stoutly that she wouldn't have given in, no matter how many drunk, angry, violent men she was facing. Ma quietly chimed in with her wise two-cents, quoting that sensible verse in Ecclesiastes: "Better a live dog than a dead lion."[27]

Uncharacteristically, Laura was horrified, exclaiming: "Oh, no, Ma! You don't mean that!" But she did mean it. . .and Ma further supported that Scriptural quote with Shakespeare's thought that "Discretion is the better part of valor."

Ma clearly valued honor. Remember that letter dated October 6, 1861 that I mentioned earlier? In it, Ma admonished her older sister to "Strive to bring [her baby boy] up to be an honor to his parents and his country." Integrity and principle were clearly fundamental personal character traits that Ma valued very deeply. Even so, there was something that could trump them. . .something she valued even more: survival.

In the whole of the *Little House* series, there are precious few examples of Laura visibly disagreeing with Ma. This scene is definitely one of them. Ma clearly felt that the practicality of surviving, even if you lose face a bit, was, and should be, the paramount objective. Laura, on the other hand, clearly felt equally strongly that she'd rather die standing up for a principle than live having abandoned it.

I admire Laura's sense of honor, but I have to side with Ma in this instance. To confront an angry, drunken crowd of hundreds of men all by yourself doesn't seem honorable to me. It seems utterly foolish. Why lose your life because other people can't understand a simple business concept? Would that sacrifice be likely to change anything? Probably not.

I think there are many causes worth losing your life over. Despite what she says in this chapter, I believe that Ma did, too. But this dispute was not one of them. I'd like to think that, because Laura was young and idealistic and had yet to have any of the

---

[27] Chapter 11, "Payday," in *By the Shores of Silver Lake*.

significant life trials that Ma had endured, she was a little overly romantic and youthfully idealistic about the situation. Ma, on the other hand, had lived a lot of life by this point. She was able to wisely discern which issues were worth a fight and which ones were better left alone.

So I stand with Ma on this issue, and admire her deeply for it. She's demonstrating a deep wisdom here, as well as a mature, practical order of priorities. She clearly places more value on the preciousness of life than in worrying about what others might think of her. I wonder what our society would be like if we did a little more of the same? I wonder what MY life might be if *I* did a little more of the same?

Robynne Elizabeth Miller

CHAPTER 10

Don't Count Your Chickens Before They're Hatched

I think most people are familiar with this old adage. And its meaning isn't particularly difficult to discern: Don't get ahead of yourself. Don't be overconfident in a thing that hasn't happened yet. Don't make plans based on something that isn't certain.

A quick internet search turns up several sites attributing the saying to Thomas Howell who, in 1570, used the phrase in his "New Sonnets and Pretty Pamphlets:"

> Counte not thy Chickens that vnhatched be,
> Waye wordes as winde, till thou finde certaintee.[28]

However, the famous Greek writer, Aesop, who lived about two thousand years before Howell (from 620 to 560 BCE!), should probably get the credit. In his (clearly modernized) fable, *The Milkmaid and Her Pail*, this wise phrase shows up at the end of a charming story:

> Patty the Milkmaid was going to market carrying her milk in a pail on her head. As she went along she began calculating what she would do with the money she would get for the milk. "I'll buy some fowls from Farmer Brown," said she, "and they will lay eggs each morning, which I will sell to the parson's wife. With the money that I get

---

[28] Martin, Gary. "Don't Count Your Chickens Before They Are Hatched - Meaning and Origin." The Phrase Finder. http://www.phrases.org.uk /meanings/count-your-chickens.html.

from the sale of these eggs I'll buy myself a new dimity frock and a chip hat; and when I go to market, won't all the young men come up and speak to me! Polly Shaw will be that jealous; but I don't care. I shall just look at her and toss my head like this. As she spoke she tossed her head back, the pail fell off it, and all the milk was spilt. So she had to go home and tell her mother what had occurred.

"Ah, my child," said the mother,

"Do not count your chickens before they are hatched."[29]

I think we've all been a little guilty of "counting our chickens" a little too soon from time to time. It's easy to sit and daydream about what we'd do if we won the lottery, or think about upgrading cars or lifestyles if we end up getting that great new job. It's fun to dream and plan and hope, and there's nothing wrong with a little optimistic fantasizing from time to time.

But it can be destructive if our planning slips from the realm of daydreams over into the realm of "taking action before something is certain." Buying a house before you have the income to actually support it, for example, isn't really wise. Nor is quitting one job in the expectation that you'll probably get the awesome one you've just interviewed for. A little "what if" session here and there, properly constrained, is no big deal. Making decisions or taking actions before you have certainty, though, well. . .that's

---

[29] Simondi, Tom. "The Milkmaid and Her Pail" Aesop's Fables Home Page. http://fablesofaesop.com/the-milkmaid-and-her-pail.html.

another story.

Ma clearly thought so, too, if out of nothing more than her sense of fatalistic practicality. Though, when she's supposed to have said this particular phrase, her intended meaning isn't abundantly clear. After a surprise rush of homesteaders who relied on the Ingalls for meals and shelter, Laura merely exclaimed "Oh, Ma! Isn't it wonderful, all the money we're making!"[30] Ma's response to Laura's excitement, though, is puzzling: "Yes, but we mustn't count chickens before they're hatched."

It's puzzling because Laura wasn't mentioning any particular goal for the money. She wasn't expecting it to go toward splashy dresses or a fancy new house or candy at a time other than Christmas. Nor was she anticipating receiving the money in the future. . .they had already netted a great deal through their make-shift restaurant and hotel business. The money was earned, received and promptly put away.

Their "eggs," so to speak, had already hatched in the form of unanticipated customers needing food and shelter. All Laura was doing, really, was expressing gratitude that they had such an unexpected and profound opportunity to earn money as the new town of De Smet was bursting into life there on the previously bare prairie.

So why did Ma throw in this comment? What chickens did she think Laura might be counting? I think the likely answer is found later in the chapter when Ma and Laura tell Pa how much money they earned in total during the spring rush. "If they could save it, Laura thought, it would be that much toward sending Mary to college." Perhaps Ma was thinking along these lines, too, though neither of them spoke it out loud.

Of course, it's also possible that Ma had no particular

---

[30] Chapter 26, "The Building Boom," in *By the Shores of Silver Lake*.

reason for saying it. She could have merely been taking the opportunity to insure that Laura didn't let her joy and excitement lead to impractical or dangerous fancies. Perhaps she was just responding to Laura's outburst of joy and excitement in a way intended to curb that emotion and bring Laura back to a calmer state. After all, Ma did like to keep her feet squarely on the ground and not get ahead of herself, now didn't she?

Either way, however, the advice was sound and fits beautifully with what we've come to know about Ma: she lived practically and decidedly in the moment. And that was quite enough for a body to handle, thank you very much!

CHAPTER 11

Pride Goes Before a Fall

In the midst of a long, frightening winter, when the trains that carried vital supplies to the lonely, remote prairie town of De Smet stopped running due to months of blizzards, Pa had to try to explain to his family why the superintendent of the railroad decided to shut down the line until spring, effectively stranding the whole town. He did his best to make the story entertaining, but the ominous implications of several more months without any more food or coal were there. The superintendent was "an easterner," Pa declared as a means of explanation. "It takes patience and perseverance to contend with things out here in the West."[31]

In a rare display of emotion, after Pa breaks the news that the trains won't run again until spring and before he begins his amusing story of the superintendent's failed attempt to clear the tracks and get the trains running, Ma is clearly both shocked and frightened at the prospect of no further incoming food or means of heat. She hears Pa state that "the superintendent ran out of patience," and exclaims:

> Patience! What's his patience got to do with it
> I'd like to know! He knows we are out here
> without supplies. How does he think we are
> going to live till spring? It isn't his business to be
> patient. It's his business to run the trains.[31]

Pa tries to soothe and encourage her before diverting everyone's attention by telling a lively version of the superintendent's story. By the time he's finished, Ma is composed

---

[31] Chapter 21, "The Hard Winter," in *The Long Winter*.

again and offers her concise assessment of this easterner's lack of knowledge and perseverance: "Pride goes before a fall."

Ma, and modern society, to be honest, have mangled the import of this saying a bit by condensing the original phrase. Staying with the theme of Biblical wisdom that Ma clearly favored, the quote is found in a passage in Scripture. Proverbs 16 states: Pride goes before destruction, a haughty spirit before a fall. (NIV) So, really, it's kind of a contraction of the two portions of the original verse.

I can't imagine the fear Ma must have felt over the possibility of her family's starvation or potential for freezing to death, nor her understandable anger toward those whose job it was to keep the trains running, but didn't. She could have, justifiably, simply belittled the superintendent. Or cried. Or yelled. Or dissolved (as I might have!) into a fit of tear-streaked hysterics. But she didn't. Instead, she used the moment to calmly drive home a difficult life lesson. . .arrogance and overconfidence often costs someone dearly. It may be the one who's prideful. Or, as in this case, it may be one or more innocent bystanders.

Ma typically guarded against over-excitement or romanticizing...partially because she felt it wasn't ladylike, but partially because she clearly believed that good judgment could easily be clouded by sentiment. Pride was a perfect example of the kind of dodgy emotion that could easily obliterate sensible thinking. Over confidence in oneself or one's abilities can lead to reckless decisions and rash choices. More often than not, these choices end badly.

So Ma recoiled from prideful people. She eschewed the values of humility and stable, steady thinking. She wasn't impressed with those who were impressed with themselves, in any way. In *Little Town on the Prairie*, for example, when Ma is getting Mary's clothes in order before she leaves for college, Laura remarks that "For once Ma did not guard against vanity" when complimenting Mary's newly made dress.[32] That's an interesting statement on two points. One is that it clearly was out of Ma's character ("for once"), and the other is the use of the word "guard." That's a fairly emotive word, isn't it?

If you guard against something, you're pretty concerned about it. You're on your toes and well aware of the potential negative consequences if you don't keep vigilant. If you're guarding something, you're protecting it, and you're likely to be willing to stretch to the point of battle if a foe presents itself. That's a mighty strong response if you're only talking about vanity.

But Ma clearly thought it was a formidable enough adversary to guard against and call out in the behavior of the foolish superintendent. And she clearly recognized the potential dangers that a vain, prideful countenance might present. At the very least, it might puff someone up to feel more valuable or important than someone else, damaging relationships and causing hurt feelings.

Somewhere in the middle, pride might give way to overconfidence, clouding sound judgment and potentially leading to rash and reckless decisions.

At the more dangerous end, however, it might leave over eighty people stranded in a blizzard weary prairie town, wondering how they were going to survive months more of winter without any further supplies of food and fuel.

No wonder Ma guarded against pride!

---

[32] Chapter 9, "Blackbirds," in *Little Town on the Prairie*.

CHAPTER 12

We Must Cut Our Coat to fit Our Cloth

I confess that this is the single most valuable lesson I learned from the *Little House* series. I love, love, LOVE it! Not only is it dripping with a profound wisdom that the modern world seems to have forgotten, but it also brings me back to the endless delightful days I spent at my beloved grandmother's work table.

A stunning seamstress, and someone who had lived through the Great Depression as a young child, she was both exquisitely creative and utterly incapable of letting something go to waste. It was a joy to sit there, snug in her sunny kitchen, quietly watching as she puzzled over and rearranged bits of leftover material from some other project. Her brow would furrow over her clear blue eyes until, suddenly, wrinkles would smooth and her smile erupt. . .she knew exactly what beautiful or useful treasures could be made from the scraps!

Ma and my grandmother were cut from the same cloth, I think, though nearly 75 years and two thousand miles apart. Neither would waste anything. Neither would stretch themselves beyond their means if at all possible. Neither bemoaned their plight, in lean years or in plenty. Both understood frugality. Deeply. But not the kind that was stingy or pinched! It was a thriftiness partially born out of circumstance and partially because it just made good sense! Why, on earth, would anybody want to waste anything?

For both my grandmother and Ma, enough was, well, *enough*. And they were grateful.

So this old proverb is particularly important to me. It connects me to my grandmother. It connects me to Ma. And it reminds me to pay more attention to the many, many blessings I have rather than to the things I might wish I had.

I can't find any early written reference to this adage, nor its certain origin. Though I did spot it on InspirationalStories.com, which has it listed under Spanish Proverbs,[33] it seems to be more universally regarded as English and appears in a few different, though very similar, permutations:

- Cut your coat according to your cloth
- You must cut your coat to fit your cloth
- Cut one's coat according to one's cloth
- We cut our coat according to our cloth
- Cut your coat to suit your cloth

Whichever way you phrase it, however, there's a whole heap of weighty wisdom in that one short little sentence. When the proverb appears, it's most typically used as a caution about finances. In that interpretation, it simply warns us to make sure our plans are appropriately related to our actual means. But it has other applications, too.

Ma used the phrase just after massive flocks of pesky blackbirds had decimated the whole year's worth of cash crops and it looked as if sending Mary to college was no longer a financial possibility for the family. But Pa and Ma had decided that it was high time for Mary to go, blackbirds or not.

So they sold a heifer. . .a move which set the farm back a whole year, for that heifer (a young cow that has not yet had a calf) would soon be a milk and butter and cheese producing machine. Both Laura and Mary were mortified at the overall cost to the family, but Ma simply reminded them: "Don't worry about it, girls.

---

[33] "Spanish Proverbs: Cut your coat according to your cloth." Inspirational Stories, Quotes & Poems. http://www.inspirationalstories.com/proverbs /spanish-cut-your-coat-according-to-your-cloth/

We must cut our coat to fit the cloth."[34]

Though the circumstance was about money in some ways, this isn't an example of paring down your plans or expectations to come into line with your means. If that had been the case, Mary's departure to the College for the Blind in Iowa would have been put off until the money to comfortably send her had been earned. No, this was the other side of that coin. In this usage, the family made a sacrifice ("cut") in order to make the goal ("coat") possible. And they did it without a hint of self-pity or complaint.

I shudder to think what either Ma or my grandmother would say about the way people today often expect more than they can afford, or are willing to sacrifice for. We don't seem to worry about putting expensive things on credit cards or purchasing houses our incomes don't really stretch to support. And not many of us consider giving up something in one area so that we can make something in another possible.

But what if we did?

What if we waited until we had the money to pay for something before we bought it? What if we chose the 40 inch TV rather than the 60 because it was the only one we could pay cash for? What if we were willing to sacrifice some comforts so that we could apply the overflow to what's really important? What if we had more money because we stopped having to pay huge interest payments each month? What if we valued the things we owned more because they cost us something valuable. . .our time or effort or something else we'd like to have had?

What would happen if we stopped putting down the coat we have to make and decided to be grateful that we had a coat at all? That's what Ma, and my grandmother, did. And what I want to do, too.

---

[34] Chapter 9, "Blackbirds," in *Little Town on the Prairie*.

My grandmother looked at a pile of material scraps and saw more than rubbish: she saw intricate quilts and darling headbands and cute-as-a-bug baby clothes. She saw *possibilities*. Similarly, Ma wasn't just demonstrating her practical side when she cut each coat, either. . .she was showing her creativity, contentment, and gratitude.

And that, most definitely, is a coat I'd like to wear!

CHAPTER 13

If wisdom's ways you wisely seek,
Five things observe with care,
To whom you speak,
Of whom you speak,
And how, and when, and where

As much as I love the thought and wisdom of the previous adage, I struggle on the opposite side of the spectrum with implementing this one! Growing up as a redhead, and a naturally verbal and emotional person, I just could not identify with Ma's calm, gentle, controlled personality. No matter how hard I tried, I just couldn't manage to consistently "modulate [my] voice" as she admonished Laura to do in Chapter 9 of *Little Town on the Prairie*. I just could not remember that "Her voice was ever gentle, low, and soft, an excellent thing in a woman." But I did try, as best I could, to at least watch WHAT I said, even if I couldn't quite control HOW I said it. And it was (read: IS) *hard*.

A number of Internet sources attribute this verse to Ma. After all, there isn't a whole lot of documentation out there to suggest otherwise. But a little very deep digging resulted in a possible find. A book called *Common School Education*, Volume 3, includes the verse in lesson 118.[35] Now, this book was published in 1889, which was eight years after Mary first went to the Iowa Braille and Sight Saving School in Vinton, Iowa. It was on that first trip to settle Mary at the school that Ma and Pa purchased the autograph albums for Laura and Carrie that eventually held Ma's rendition of this verse.

In the *Common School Education* book, Lesson 118 is

---

[35] Badlam, Anna B. "Lesson 118. Board-Work for the Teacher." In *Common School Education*, 388. Vol. 3. Eastern Educational Bureau, 1889.

called "Board-Work for the Teacher" and was copyrighted in 1888 by the author, Anna B. Badlam. Although this lesson was written and published years after Ma wrote in Laura's album, I rather highly doubt that Anna had managed in the interim years to sneak a peek into that album and plagiarize Ma's original verse. Possible, of course, but highly unlikely.

No, I think the more likely chronology of events is that this verse had either been handed down verbally through the generations far predating Ma and Laura, or was an actual written verse in some tome we've yet to discover. If we doubt the possibility that Ms. Badlam stole it from Ma for the purpose of writing her lesson, we have to believe that the verse was commonly known. This would, of course, dispel the widespread belief that Ma actually wrote it.

Whatever the actual origin, though, Ma's decision to write it down for Laura was a pretty good one. Laura had grown frustrated with a prideful and mean spirited girl (Nellie!), and had occasionally let a curt or caustic word slip out of her mouth. Those words inflamed the already ridiculous Nellie to even greater efforts to hurt and defame Laura to their schoolteacher, Miss Wilder. The ensuing chaos resulted in utter disruption at school, the threat of expulsion, accusations of impropriety levied, and an eventual visit from the school board (on which Pa sat!).

After that school board visit, back in the comfort of their own home, Pa asked Laura to tell her side of what had happened and to explain why Miss Wilder had gotten such a twisted view of Laura's character and beliefs. Laura had been preparing to defend herself against a lie that Miss Wilder had told about her, but wasn't prepared to look for the potential reason behind Miss Wilder's opinion. Laura told her story, and eventually made the connection between some things that she had said in anger to Nellie Oleson and the eventual untruths that Nellie then planted in Miss Wilder's mind.

After the whole story was out, Ma responded:

> "Oh, Laura," Ma said sorrowfully. "That made her angry."[36]

A short while later, Ma asked Laura to go get her Autograph Album so she could write in it. The verse was short and simple, but packed with import:

> If wisdom's ways you wisely seek,
> Five things observe with care,
> To whom you speak,
> Of whom you speak,
> And how, and when, and where

Ma, herself, sought wisdom. As we've already learned, she did it through staying in the moment, keeping her emotions in check, and maintaining an attitude of humility. But here's another piece, too: She did it by keeping control of her words.

Control. Of. Her. Words.

Sigh. So hard, and yet, such a powerful concept. Well, actually, FIVE powerful concepts!

If we choose to make sure that we only speak with people whom we can trust, we'd certainly be a lot better off. We obviously can't go quietly through life, remaining silent to everyone who isn't our best friend, but we can choose to keep intimate or important thoughts reserved for those who will care for and respect our words and emotions.

Likewise, we can choose to be VERY careful about whom

---

[36] Chapter 15, "The School Board's Visit," in *Little Town on the Prairie*.

we speak. Ma was undoubtedly very familiar with the Scriptures cautioning us against gossip (1 Tim. 5:13-14 and 2 Cor. 12:20, for example). Not only does gossip often hurt those who are gossiped about, but it also reveals the character of the one who gossips. A person who cannot say kind words about others, who cannot be trusted with private information, or who takes pleasure in spreading hurtful information is diminishing their own chances for meaningful relationships. After all, who wants to be connected with someone mean, untrustworthy, and hurtful?

The "how" bit of Ma's poem used to puzzle me. As a young girl, I thought maybe it had something to do with tone of voice. As I grew older, I learned that it has a great deal more to do with your motivation than anything else. If, for example, you share with someone that a mutual friend seems sad and your heart is to help and brainstorm how to make things better, that's a far different scenario from simply telling someone your mutual friend is depressed AGAIN and is someone to avoid if you don't want to get bummed out, too.

Though I'm pretty sure that tone of voice, posture, and body language were at least partially what Ma was referring to, as well. How you speak to someone (with respect and politeness) can go a long way toward making whatever you have to say more palatable to the hearer. All four of my kids have heard numerous mom-lectures that go something like: Being angry is okay. Being rude because of your anger is not.

When and where you speak to someone is probably equal parts considering the actual time you choose to talk and whether you're really ready to speak at all. Ma waited to speak until she was calm and ready to say something from a place of rationality. She chose, time and time again, to make sure she was clear headed and ready to talk before she actually did.

Likewise, she plainly thought that choosing the right

opportunity, in the right location was important. Working out a quarrel in the middle of Main Street wouldn't have been the right time OR place to have such a discussion. Nor was it the right time for Laura to address Nellie: in the brief moments before classes began, when Laura was angry and shocked and emotional.

It's easier said than done, though, isn't it? No doubt Ma's naturally calm personality helped. But even the more emotional and expressive among us can benefit from realizing that it's the choices we actively make each time we speak that can make a significant difference.

I want that ability. . .to easily make the right choices at the right time. To carefully consider to whom I am speaking, of whom I am speaking, and how and when and where. I'm sure those around me would appreciate my efforts in that direction. And, of course, Ma would, too.

Robynne Elizabeth Miller

CHAPTER 14

A Body Makes His Own Luck

This adage has traveled with me ever since I first read those words as a young girl. I honestly didn't get it back then. I mean, luck was, by definition, totally independent of anything we could do for ourselves. Wasn't it?

That's the whole point of luck, I thought, be it good or bad: it just randomly happens to you. Later, I came to understand that Ma wasn't redefining the concept of luck. . .she was making a bold declaration that she didn't believe it really existed.

In *These Happy Golden Years*, Laura was fussing over a recently earned teaching certificate, hoping that she could "only have the good luck to get the right school." Ma quickly (though placidly!) responded to her: "A body makes his own luck, be it good or bad."[37] Laura was as puzzled as I was, wondering later that same chapter "how to make herself the good luck to get the one she wanted."

I did quite a bit of research into the origin of the phrase, but couldn't locate an exact replica. Eventually, I had to come to the conclusion that Ma was probably paraphrasing a concept that had been around for ages. There are wagonloads of quotes related to luck, and many of them have extremely similar meanings, though quite different phrasings. Here's a sampling:

- Chance favors the prepared mind – Louis Pasteur
- Diligence is the mother of good luck – Benjamin Franklin
- I'm a great believer in luck, and I find the harder

---

[37] Chapter 26, "Teachers' Examinations," in *These Happy Golden Years*.

I work, the more I have of it – Thomas Jefferson
- Everyone is the author of his own good fortune (French)
- Everyone is the maker of his own fate (English)
- Fortune helps them that help themselves (English)

So, even if Ma's exact quote doesn't predate her, the concept certainly does. And it's another good one. It takes the onus off of a random universe and puts our destiny largely back into our own hands. . .which is right where it should be. But how do we *make* good luck?

Ma seemed to divide that which happens in our lives into two categories. . .the stuff that we have control over and the stuff we don't. Some people might point to the second category as the birth place of luck. I'm not sure Ma would have agreed. The stuff we don't have control over, she would likely argue, are environments, be them nature or man-made. And both have a rhythm and pattern that is logical, set, and outside any whims or fancies. In *Little Town on the Prairie*, Chapter 22, for example, Laura and Ma have the following conversation:

> "I don't see how anybody can be prepared for anything," said Laura. "When you expect something, and then something else always happens."
>
> "Laura," said Ma.
>
> "Well, it does, Ma," Laura protested.
>
> "No," Ma said. "Even the weather has more sense in it than you seem to give it credit for. Blizzards come only in a blizzard country. You may be well prepared to teach school and

still not be a schoolteacher, but if you are not prepared, it's certain that you won't be."

Ma is making a strong delineation here between what we can control (our own actions, choices, and preparedness) and that which we can't (blizzards, environments, natural phenomenon, etc.). But even the things out of control have a "sense" in them. We may be surprised at an unforeseen blizzard, Ma might argue, but it shouldn't be regarded as "bad luck." Blizzards come in blizzard country. Whether we are watchful and prepared is our lookout. We can't blame nature for working the way it does.

To put it in a modern framework, I have a friend who once visited a particularly poor area in an already desperately impoverished country. She was pressed on all sides, wherever she went, with beggars and could hardly move through the streets to her destinations. She was frustrated that it was such a struggle to complete her reasons for being there (which were very good ones!) and became almost angry that the tasks for which she had come might be partially left undone. Her team leader finally took her aside and reminded her that this environment was well known, and had been expected. It wasn't "bad luck" to be hindered from movement this way. . .it was an expected, natural occurrence where they were.

What we do have control over, however, is our own preparedness. Ma was right to advise Laura that, even if she was prepared, she might never be a schoolteacher. But if she wasn't prepared, on the other hand, it was certain that she wouldn't be. We need to ready ourselves for whatever opportunities arise, in whatever way we can: physically, academically, and socially.

But that doesn't quite answer the question: how do we make our own luck? Beyond being prepared for something, I believe Ma was teaching Laura that our relationships with others has a great deal to do with our "good luck." We've all heard the modern adage "it's who you know that counts" and have probably bemoaned our own poor connections to the school or job or opportunity we were after. Yet, sitting at home, waiting for opportunity, or going into the community with a poor attitude or rubbish work ethic, is not exactly going to produce terribly good results, now is it?

Laura was being kind when she befriended Florence Wilkins. She didn't know then that Florence had a connection to any school. . .she just knew she "looks nice, and she looks lonesome,"[38] and so decided to go talk to her. That kind gesture to a shy new girl in school, and their resulting friendship, made the "luck" that Laura needed later when Florence had influence on who would get to teach at a large school near her home. Florence had experienced Laura's kindness, got a chance to see her character and abilities, and knew she'd be a perfect fit for the job.

Laura didn't do anything fancy. She certainly had no ulterior motive when she made friends with Florence, but that gesture demonstrated her character and gave an opportunity for Florence to get to know who Laura was and what her hopes were. That's the kind of "luck making" Ma was talking about: Be prepared, understand the natural cadence of an environment, and treat others with kindness and respect. If you do all of those things diligently, sooner or later, Ma would reason, something good is bound to happen! Lucky, huh??

---

[38] Chapter 22, "Singing School," in *These Happy Golden Years*.

CHAPTER 15

Marry in Haste, Repent in Leisure
Married in Black, You'll Wish Yourself Back

I'm not surprised that Ma was given an opportunity to chime in on the subject of marriage. Almost all of the adages and proverbs attributed to Ma throughout the *Little House* series were solid life lessons, applicable to just about any circumstance a person might face. But marriage was, and still should be, a particularly important and sober-minded endeavor.

Even in today's rather immediate-gratification-and-wanting-things-to-be-easy society, where marriages are entered into quickly and ended almost equally so, there are, at the very least, huge financial and familial implications in choosing to legally bind yourself to another. Ma would have added that there's a significant moral component, too, though that's not a particularly popular modern notion. So it's no wonder Laura made sure that Ma weighed in on the subject!

The first of two marriage-related statements, made just a few paragraphs apart in Chapter 21: Wedding Plans of *These Happy Golden Years*, has been erroneously attributed to Samuel Johnson. For example, Patt Morrison, in an online article titled "Just Who is the Audience for Princeton Mom's College-Girl Advice?" (written for the L.A. Times), believed: "The English writer and critic Samuel Johnson minted that phrase 'Marry in Haste, Repent in Leisure.'"[39] But Samuel lived from 1709-1784, and yet the earliest written record of the old saying is in William Congreve's 1693 comedy of manners *The Old Batchelour*, in

---

[39] Morrison, Patt. "Just Who Is the Audience for Princeton Mom's College-girl Advice?" Los Angeles Times. March 20, 2014. http://www.latimes.com/opinion/opinion-la/la-ol-princeton-moms-college-girl-advice-20140319-story.html.

which he writes:

> Thus grief still treads upon the heels of pleasure:
> Married in haste, we may repent at leisure.

So, though Mr. Johnson may have *repeated* the proverb, and possibly was the one who brought it more fully into the public eye, he certainly wasn't the one who should get the writing credit!

The second of the two phrases is taken from an old poem on marriage, though I could not discover its actual origin:

> Married in White, you have chosen right
> Married in Grey, you will go far away,
> Married in Black, you will wish yourself back,
> Married in Red, you will wish yourself dead,
> Married in Green, ashamed to be seen,
> Married in Blue, you will always be true,
> Married in Pearl, you will live in a whirl,
> Married in Yellow, ashamed of your fellow,
> Married in Brown, you will live in the town,
> Married in Pink, your spirit will sink.[40]

Personally, I think that whoever actually wrote this poem had a little too much time on their hands and merely liked the process of rhyming, as there isn't a whole lot of solid logic behind it. But a lot of people back in the day bought into these kinds of wedding superstitions. . .just in case.

When Laura told her family that she would be married to

---

[40] "Wedding Superstitions You May Not Know About." ItThing.com. http://itthing.com/wedding-superstitions.

Almanzo much sooner than originally planned, and would wear the new black cashmere dress they were making, she feared that Ma would think she was marrying in haste, and could hear her mother quoting the worrying proverb in her head. But their reasons were sound. . .to do so would show good financial sense in their particular circumstances. Plus, Laura and Almanzo had been going together for about three years at this point, so it wasn't really in haste, was it?

Ma didn't actually end up questioning the timing of the marriage in the book, though it's interesting that Laura made sure that Ma's belief about entering into the covenant of marriage did make an appearance. Clearly, Ma had instilled in her daughters the notion that marriage was a serious endeavor requiring careful consideration and control over emotions which could cloud judgment or rush the important decision. Ma did, however, worry a bit over the color of the wedding dress.

> "I do not like to think of your being married in black," said Ma. "You know what they say, 'Married in black, you'll wish yourself back.'"[41]

In response, Laura cheerfully reassured her:

> It will be new. I will wear my old sage-green poke bonnet with the blue silk lining, and borrow your little square gold pin with the strawberry in it, so I'll be wearing something old and something new, something borrowed and something blue.

---

[41] Chapter 21, "Wedding Plans," in *These Happy Golden Years*.

Ma finally consented, admitting that she didn't "suppose there's any truth in these old sayings."

I love that we get to see a bit of whimsy in Ma again here. There's not a lot of it to be found throughout the series! That she even considered giving any credence to a superstitious belief about marriage shows that she did have at least a small spark of imagination, despite her quickly extinguishing it with her final practical statement on the matter.

Plus, it's the first attributed statement that reveals more about Ma's real personality. Even though Ma didn't actually warn Laura not to "Marry in Haste," Laura had clearly heard her mother say it enough to know it was her firm belief on the subject. And it fits in well with what we know about Ma, doesn't it?

Ma was a steady, dependable realist. She thought that romantic notions and unchecked emotions lent nothing of value to the making of sound, sensible decisions. She also believed that marriage was, and should be, a final decision. So it's not surprising that she thought such a serious and irrevocable resolution should be made slowly and with exquisitely careful consideration. With all we know about her character, it's no stretch to think of Ma weighing up the practical pros and cons about joining her life and future to another human being very, very cautiously, and believing that others (especially her daughters!) should, as well.

Does this mean that I don't think she had romantic love for Charles? No. I think she deeply cared for him as well as their daughters. But I do think that love was not enough for her to make a decision to marry Charles. I think she believed that Charles was a capable provider, a moral man, and a dependable leader for their future family. Whether all that actually turned out to be true is a matter of discussion. . .but Ma clearly believed it when she carefully decided to join her life to his. And it's certainly what Ma wanted for her daughters, as well.

Think carefully, decide slowly, and, hopefully, you won't live to regret it!

CHAPTER 16

They That Dance Must Pay the Fiddler

Hardcore fans of the *Little House* series know that *The First Four* years was merely an unfinished draft chronicling the early part of Laura's marriage to Almanzo. It wasn't complete or polished or remotely intended for publication at the time of Laura's death in 1957 (just three days past her 90th birthday!!). Laura is largely regarded to have written the manuscript around 1940, but lost interest in the project soon after, possibly due to the failing health of her beloved husband or simply due to her own age and health issues.

The draft wasn't even discovered until Laura's daughter, Rose Wilder Lane, passed away in 1968 and her executor found it amongst some of her papers. In 1971, that executor, Roger Lea McBride, decided to publish the work without any editing or polishing (except for correcting a few spelling errors!).

I give this background because *The First Four Years* has a couple of themes not exactly in keeping with a series meant for children. Some have speculated, seeing as *These Happy Golden Years* was published in 1943 with a note at the end saying "The end of the Little House books," that Laura never intended *The First Four Years* as anything other than a personal family history. Another theory is that she might have intended the project as a stand alone novel for adults. Otherwise, why would the "end" note have been included at the conclusion of *These Happy Golden Years*? That book was published several years after *The First Four Years* was supposed to have been written, so if Laura had already written a ninth *Little House* book, putting "the end" after the eighth just wouldn't have made sense. Furthermore, those *First Four Years* themes were decidedly NOT for children and certainly weren't a logical culmination to the overall *Little House* story arc.

Whatever Laura's reason for penning (or, penciling, rather!) this draft, we have our first tiny (shocking?) "Little House" glimpse into the subject of sex.

Laura found herself suddenly and exceptionally ill in the first year of marriage. "For days she fainted whenever she left her bed. The doctor told her to lie quietly. He assured her she would feel much better before long and that in a few months, nine to be exact, she would be quite all right. Laura was going to have a baby."[42]

But, though Laura was hard hit by morning (and day and night!) sickness, she didn't let her condition keep her from doing her share. "As she went so miserably about her work she would smile wryly now and then as she remembered a saying of her mother's: 'They that dance must pay the fiddler.'"

Obviously, it's not a raunchy, tasteless, gratuitous reference, but given Laura's prim nature and conservative outlook, it's a fairly strong statement. Laura and Almanzo had enjoyed their new marital relationship and, unsurprisingly, pregnancy (and it's hormonally induced down side of unpleasant symptoms) was the result.

The original expression isn't actually related to romantic relations. . .Laura just cheekily commandeered it for that purpose. The real meaning is basically this: If you get a benefit from something, you can also expect to have to pay the associated costs.

Sources claim the origin is likely either Scottish or English and the proverb has many variations:

> A check into the standard proverb collections reveals that this is actually a shortened version of such proverbs as "Who pays the piper, calls the

---

[42] Chapter 1, "The First Year," in *The First Four Years*.

> tune" (1611), "Those that dance must pay the music" (1638), "He who pays the piper may order the tune" and "He who pays the piper can call the tune," for which 1611 is the earliest reference, but which are probably older.[43]

And:

> In its figurative sense the English phrase dates back to Thomas Flat-man's [sic] *Heraclitus ridens* (1681): "After all this Dance he has led the Nation, he must at least come to pay the Piper himself."[44]

Despite the way Laura used the proverb, I kind of like that this was a saying of Ma's. I like that she didn't expect to have someone else provide her pleasures for her, romantic or otherwise. She clearly expected that a person should "pay" for whatever they benefited from, whether it was through hard work, sacrifice, or cash money.

How much different would our society be today if we believed this, too?

Why? Because I think Ma knew something that we don't: Paying your own way in life isn't only fair. . .it actually instills in us a sort of self-confidence born out of using our own abilities. If she ever allowed the use of the word "pride," I think this would be

---

[43] Okebalama, Dozie. "Reuben Abati and German Piper of Hamelin." National Mirror. June 19, 2015. http://nationalmirroronline.net/new/reuben-abati-and-german-piper-of-hamelin/.

[44] Hill, Karen. "Where Does the Phrase 'to Pay the Fiddler (or Piper)' Come From and What Does It Mean?" Super Beefy. June 1, 2014. http://superbeefy.com /where-does-the-phrase-to-pay-the-fiddler-or-piper-come-from-and-what-does-it-mean/.

a good time. If we sacrifice for something, or work hard to earn something, or even build something of our very own, we can have the (healthy) sense of pride that comes from providing for our own needs and pleasures.

I think Ma embodied that idea. She had the satisfaction of knowing her family wore clothes that she made and repaired, ate food she largely grew and prepared from scratch, and used things she created with her own two hands (quilts, pillows, pin cushions, needle books, bed shoes, etc.). Every stitch, every mouthful, and every use was made/provided/given with a profound amount of love.

We rob ourselves of that satisfaction when we don't pay our own fiddlers. We reduce things and people and blessings to less than they could be when we repeatedly reap what we don't sow. And that is most certainly a shame.

In Laura's case, she had to address that old fiddler whether she intended to or not. Yet, armed with Ma's old saying and belief that we're responsible to pay for whatever we receive, she did so without self-pity or hint of anger. Queasy tummy and all!

CONCLUSION

When I started this project, I had a few preconceived notions about Ma. Or perhaps, I hate to admit, they were more like prejudices. I felt distant from Ma, and confused, as well. Laura seemed to love and respect her deeply on the one hand. On the other, she depicted her character in such a way as to keep her almost at arm's-length from us and slightly out of focus.

But Ma was there, wasn't she? Amongst the cheese hoops and mending clothes and making sure her daughters received a decent education. What seemed stiff and a little formal to me before I began the research for this book now seems more like character traits I'd like to have: resolve, practicality, fortitude and an enduring sense of gratitude for each day and every blessing.

I can see, too, how it all began. To lose your beloved father, and to have your entire world and sense of security ripped from you through one tragic event, is almost unimaginable for adults who have money in the bank and the maturity to process such loss and fear. But Ma was just a little girl when her life was turned upside-down. Yet she didn't crumble.

I deeply admire her for that.

Modern relationship experts often talk about our Love Languages. . .the way we express love to each other and best receive it for ourselves. Ma doesn't speak my Love Language. Mine is covered in mud from impromptu puddle jumping sessions and disheveled from exciting kitchen competitions à la Food Network's *Chopped*. It's full of cuddles and sticky faces and an endless stream of "I love you more than the moon and the stars."

So Ma's Love Language doesn't look a thing like mine. Hers was expressed through quiet, unwavering devotion and service to her family, her insistence on formal education, her personal sacrifice of comforts, and her continual desire to teach her four girls life's most important and valuable lessons.

It may not have been as obvious as the frequent kisses I smother my babies with, but it's obvious nonetheless. Ma's devotion to her family permeated every task, sacrifice, and teaching opportunity. And it never seemed to waver.

Was she perfect? Of course not. Though I kind of like that, to be honest. Her imperfections make her relatable. More real. Would I like her to be a little less caustic on the subject of Native Americans and foreigners? Sure. And do I still have a bit of trouble with the prairie fire scene in which getting cleaned up seems to take precedence over comforting little Laura? Well, yes, I do.

But there's so much more in the "I wish I were like Ma" column than otherwise, isn't there? While I'm rushing about like a maniacal and unpaid taxi driver, I wish I had her sense of calm and order. And wouldn't it be nice to know that the household washing would be done each Monday and that fresh bread was a given on Saturday?

And what about her practicality? I love that she lived firmly in the moment, not counting her chickens before they hatched. But I love even more that she was intentional about cutting her coats to fit her cloth. Satisfied with enough, and without a hint of self-pity, Ma's "coats" were not only practical and realistic. . .they were also drenched in a sense of contentment and gratitude. A beautiful way to live.

Her fortitude, however, is what I most deeply appreciate and respect. Life threw so many ugly curve balls at her, yet she remained dignified, graceful, and resilient no matter what. A plague of grasshoppers destroying a year's labor and income? At least the chickens have feed! Pesky blackbirds descend by the thousands? Make blackbird pie!

Could you have reacted like that? I'm not sure I could. But, then again, you never know until you're tested.

Ma *was* tested. Time and time again. Through catastrophic natural disasters, devastating illnesses, near poverty, and through the simple realities of trying to carve a life out of harsh, unpredictable environments.

We're removed from all that, you and I. Oh, I know we experience personal tragedies and periods of financial strain. And I certainly know the pain of loss and grief, as most of us will at some point. But can we ever understand the reality of working hard just to have enough to eat and enough fuel to keep us from freezing in the winter? Will we ever face financial ruin if one year's crop doesn't flourish? Will we ever try to stick it out in a one-board-thick building while months of below-zero blizzards howl outside?

Probably not. We're pretty lucky, you and I.

So my heart has turned a little more toward Ma. I have no frame of reference for living in the harsh environment or time period she did. I have no way of understanding how stressful it can be to live in the constant fear of starvation and financial ruin. I have no way of relating to how a family's livelihood, prosperity, and even survival could be so tenuously linked to weather, insects, and even the pridefulness of an eastern railroad superintendent.

But Ma sure did.

And it's time I stopped comparing her to the modern standard of a loving mother. Modern moms have dishwashers and Walmarts and way too many clothes in our wardrobes. We can shove a load of laundry into a tub and simply push a button to complete the washing process while we go off to read our babies bedtime stories. We buy our butter and eggs and milk and replace whatever we need to through a quick trip to the nearby store. We don't grow and raise and hunt for our food, make our own clothes and homes and furniture, or cook over an open fire.

But if this was the circumstance of my life, I hope I'd be able to navigate it with the grace and strength Ma seemed to. Her words, actions, and legacy challenge and encourage me.

I hope they do the same for you.

ABOUT THE AUTHOR

Robynne Elizabeth Miller is wife to an amazing Brit, mother to a glorious brood of adopted and biological kids, and makes her home in the snowy woods of Northern California's Sierra Nevada Mountains.

Passionate about her family, faith, music and cooking, she can also be found blogging at mylittleprairiehome.com and thepracticalpioneer.com.

Email: robynne@thepracticalpioneer.com

Web: mylittleprairiehome.com

            thepracticalpioneer.com

Twitter: @mlprairiehome

Pinterest: pinterest.com/mlprairiehome/

Made in the USA
Lexington, KY
21 June 2018